Grilled Cheese
at
Four O'Clock in
the Morning

Grilled Cheese
at
Four O'Clock in
the Morning

by Judy Miller

illustrations by Jeanne Turner

A publication of the **American Diabetes Association**®

For my son Alan

Contents

Foreward

The American Diabetes Association is pleased to present *Grilled Cheese at Four O'Clock in the Morning*. This novel for young people aged eight to twelve is a first for us. We think it's a unique way to present some important information. We're sure that many young people who are diagnosed with diabetes will be able to identify with Scott, the main character in the book. In learning to cope with his diabetes, Scott learns some important lessons about himself and life. We hope you'll learn something, too.

John A. Colwell, M.D., Ph.D.
President
American Diabetes Association
1987–1988

Preface

The idea for *Grilled Cheese at Four O'Clock in the Morning* came from helping my own son learn to live with diabetes. Although my son Alan was diagnosed at a much younger age than Scott, the main character in this book, he experienced many of the same feelings of anger and frustration before accepting the reality of diabetes. The title of the book also came from personal experience. I always fix Alan a grilled cheese sandwich when he has a nighttime insulin reaction, and those reactions usually occur at about four o'clock in the morning.

I would like to extend special thanks to the following people: Luther Travis, M.D., Professor of Pediatrics and Director, Divisions of Nephrology/Diabetes, and Barbara Schreiner, R.N., M.N., C.D.E., Diabetes Nurse Specialist, at the University of Texas Medical Branch in Galveston, for their ongoing involvement as the manuscript developed—their expert advice was invaluable; Maysil Malard, R.N., C.D.E., for her shared insights into family dynamics; Frank Haynes, for suggesting the title; Nicky Schulz, for reviewing and proofreading; Alain Taylon, M.D., for his information on developmental issues; Mary Ann Keller, R.N., M.S., C.D.E., for her help in bringing the manuscript to the attention of the American Diabetes Association

Committee on Publications; and Arthur Krosnick, M.D., and Sandra F. Epstein, A.C.S.W., for reviewing the manuscript.

This book was produced with contributions from the staff of the American Diabetes Association National Service Center, in particular Robin M. Scott, Janice T. Radak, Susan H. Coughlin, and Caroline A. Stevens.

ONE
Nobody Cares

S cott leaped out of bed, his brown hair standing straight up as he pulled an old soccer
T-shirt over his head. He grinned when he yanked
open the drapes and looked out at the sunny, wind-
less day. *Great,* he thought, *a perfect day for
soccer.*

Suddenly the smile left his face, and he slumped
down on the bed. He remembered. Everything

was ruined now—soccer, sixth grade—everything! Scott lay back and stared at the ceiling. *It's just not fair,* he thought.

"Scott! Are you up?" Mom's voice floated up from the kitchen. "Breakfast is almost ready."

"I'm coming," he answered. Ever since he'd come home from the hospital, Mom was constantly checking on him. Scott started down the stairs, one step at a time. "Why can't everybody just leave me alone?" he muttered.

Mom was standing by the counter buttering toast, an apron covering her skirt and blouse. "I'll be at work this morning," she said, "so I fixed a sandwich for your lunch. It's in the refrigerator."

Scott nodded. "I can fix my own lunch," he said.

Melissa wandered into the kitchen, yawning and stretching. Sometimes people thought she and Mom were sisters because of their matching blue eyes and curly blond hair.

"What are you doing up?" Mom asked.

"Cheerleading practice," Melissa answered. "The juniors have to teach the routines to the new squad members."

"I'm glad you both have morning practices," Mom said. "Then you'll be in the habit of getting up on time when school starts next week."

After breakfast, Mom followed Scott into the

hallway. ''Scott, I know we've talked about this before, but have you decided to tell any of your friends about having diabetes?'' she asked. ''It's been three weeks since you left the hospital.''

''No,'' he answered. ''You're not going to tell anyone, are you? No one needs to know.''

''You might feel better if you told someone. I'm sure Chris would understand.''

''Maybe,'' Scott replied, dashing out the door before she could say any more. He waited at the corner for Chris for several minutes and then headed for the school without him. *I suppose I could tell Chris,* he thought. *He's my best friend.*

''Hey, Scott! Wait up!'' Chris came running up the street, pushing his glasses up on his nose as he ran. ''I had to go back and get the guard strap for my glasses,'' he explained. ''Otherwise, they fall off all the time.''

When they arrived at the school, Chris ran and joined two other early arrivals practicing dribbling and juggling. Scott plopped down and stared at his shoes. *I'll never really have any fun again,* he thought, *unless this diabetes goes away.*

A few minutes later, Coach Rollins arrived. He joined the boys practicing on the field, his tall frame bent as he easily dribbled the ball down the field, past the defenders, and into the goal. He tapped Chris lightly on the shoulder. ''Now you try it,'' he said.

The coach came over to where Scott was sitting. ''How's it going?'' he asked. ''I noticed on your sports physical that you were recently diagnosed with diabetes. If you need to stop and drink some juice or rest, go ahead. I'll understand. Okay?''

''Okay,'' Scott answered.

''I hope you're feeling all right. Having diabetes isn't easy.'' Coach Rollins turned toward the field. ''We'll get started in a minute,'' he said, walking away.

Is that it? Scott thought. *Boy, a lot he cares!* He walked onto the field when the coach blew his whistle for practice to start.

After a few minutes of drills, the coach blew his whistle again. ''Now that everyone's warmed up,'' he announced, ''we'll scrimmage for awhile.'' He quickly divided the players into two teams and began assigning positions.

Scott ran to the center of the field. Like everyone else, he wanted to play forward because forwards usually made the goals. *Since Coach Rollins knows I have diabetes,* Scott thought, *he'll probably want to do something special for me today, and he'll let me play forward.*

''Scott,'' Coach Rollins said, ''you'll be goalie the first half.''

Nobody Cares

Scott stopped and turned toward the coach. "I think I should get to play forward," he said.

Coach Rollins's eyebrows drew together, and he frowned, but he looked more puzzled than angry. "I know," he said, "but so does everyone else. You're quick with your hands and have the potential to be an excellent goalie."

"Playing goalie is boring," Scott mumbled. He shoved his fists into his jeans' pockets, turned his back on the rest of the team, and walked toward the sidelines. When he reached the edge of the field, he stopped. *Maybe I'll just go on home,* he thought. *Who needs this game, anyway?* He jumped slightly when Coach Rollins laid a hand on his shoulder. He hadn't realized the coach had followed him off the field.

Coach Rollins spoke softly. "You know, Scott, if you want to play soccer, you're expected to play all the positions." He paused a moment, then looked Scott straight in the eye. "I'm sorry you have diabetes, but you can't expect special treatment all your life because of it." He paused again, then leaned down and picked up a shirt laying on the ground. "Here's the goalie's jersey," he said, holding out the shirt.

Scott slowly reached out, took the shirt and slid it over his head. He walked toward the goal with his head down, fists again jammed into his pockets. When practice ended, he dropped the goalie's jersey and started home without Chris.

As he left the field, he passed Coach Rollins talking to a tall, dark-haired boy that Scott had never seen before. ''We'll be glad to have you on the team, Dirk,'' the coach said. ''We can use another good goalie.''

Scott looked up when he heard the coach's comment. *He's probably ready to replace me already,* Scott thought. *Nobody wants a goalie with diabetes.*

Chris caught up with Scott about halfway home. ''Why didn't you want to play goalie?'' he asked.

''It's not fair,'' Scott answered.

''Not fair?'' Chris asked. ''Coach Rollins makes everyone play all the positions. You know that. Besides, you're our best goalie.''

Scott hesitated, then said, ''I mean it's not fair having diabetes.''

Chris stared at Scott. ''What are you talking about?'' he asked.

''I have diabetes,'' Scott answered. ''I was in the hospital for three days when you were on vacation.''

Chris's eyes opened wide. ''What happened?'' he asked.

''It's kind of confusing,'' Scott admitted, ''but,

for some reason, my body has quit making insulin. You have to have insulin or you'll die, so I have to take two shots of insulin every day.''

''Is this a joke?'' Chris asked.

''No!'' Scott said. ''It's no joke.''

''Do you feel sick?''

''Not really,'' Scott said. ''But I just hate it! And I can't eat candy or ice cream ever again.''

''Are you sure you're not kidding?'' Chris asked as they reached Scott's house.

''I'm sure,'' Scott said. ''Come on in. I'll prove it to you.''

Scott started by showing Chris his syringes. ''See this little needle?'' he said. ''After I put the insulin in the syringe, I grab a place on my arm or leg and stick the needle in.''

''Doesn't that hurt?'' asked Chris.

''Not too much,'' Scott answered. ''You get used to it. Then you break off the needle and throw both pieces away.''

''But how do you know how much insulin to use?'' Chris asked.

''Well, I take a set amount, but I test my blood just to make sure it's right,'' Scott said. ''Come on in the bathroom—I'll show you how I test my blood.''

Chris followed. ''What are you talking about?''

''I have to test my blood every day,'' Scott said,

handing Chris a small machine.

"You can't trick me. This is some kind of calculator."

"It is not!" Scott took the machine. "See this little needle? I use it to prick my finger."

"I don't believe it!" Chris turned and started to leave the room.

"Wait," Scott said. "I'll do a test and prove it."

Chris stopped and turned back.

"Look," Scott said. He used the automatic lancet to prick his finger. He squeezed his finger slightly and a large drop of blood appeared.

Chris leaned over to get a closer look. "What are you going to do now?" he asked.

"The blood goes on the pad on the end of this stick," Scott explained. "Then I wait until the machine beeps, blot the stick, and put it in the machine."

Chris watched silently while Scott did the procedure.

"Now I wait until the machine beeps again and then it'll tell what my blood sugar is. I have to write each one down in this book."

"How often do you have to stick your finger and do the test?" Chris asked.

"I'm supposed to check it three or four times a day," Scott explained.

"I still don't get it. What does the number on

the machine mean?''

"Well, it tells if my blood sugar is high or low. If I don't eat enough, it goes too low."

"Then what happens?" Chris asked.

"I get shaky and dizzy," Scott explained, "and I have to have some sugar."

"What if you don't get any sugar when you get low?''

"I guess I pass out," Scott answered. "It hasn't happened. Mom watches me all the time."

"Mothers always worry," Chris agreed. "But what happens if your blood sugar gets too high?''

"Then I have to do another kind of test for ketones to see if I need extra insulin. And if it's high a lot of the time, Dr. Carrington will change my daily insulin dose. Or he might tell me to get more exercise.''

Chris left, and Scott put away his machine. *I'm glad I told Chris,* he thought. *You shouldn't keep secrets from your best friend.*

TWO
Decisions

S cott woke up early the first day of school and was in the kitchen for breakfast before Dad and Melissa. He took his insulin out of the cupboard and sat down at the table to do his injection.

Mom was standing at the counter, still in her bathrobe, making sandwiches. "What kind of sandwich do you want in your lunch, Scott?" she asked, as she watched Scott measure his insulin.

Decisions

"I'm going to take hot lunch, just like last year," Scott said. He rolled up his sleeve and injected his insulin.

Mom came over and sat down at the table. "I don't know if that's a good idea," she said. "Hot lunch might not have the right amounts of what you need to eat for your diabetes."

"You can get seconds on bread," Scott explained. "And they always have some kind of fruit. I know what I'm supposed to have."

Mom thought a minute. "Maybe you could ask for a copy of the menu each week, and then we could plan ahead."

"I guess I could ask Mrs. Schaeffer for a menu. She's one of the cooks." Scott ate his breakfast, then jumped up and ran to find his schoolbag.

Mom's voice followed him. "I expect you to clear and rinse your own dishes," she said.

I'll pretend I didn't hear her, Scott decided. *Since I have to do all this other stuff in the morning for diabetes, the least she can do is pick up my dishes.* He grabbed his schoolbag and ran out the door.

Chris was waiting at the corner. "We'd better be on time," he said. "I hear Mrs. Whitney is really strict about kids being tardy."

"She knows about my diabetes," Scott said. "I hope she doesn't say anything to the rest of the kids in the class.''

Lincoln School was the smallest of the eight elementary schools in Beech, and Scott knew most of the other sixth graders from last year. But as Mrs. Whitney called roll, she introduced the boy Scott had seen talking to Coach Rollins at soccer practice. ''I know most of you from seeing you on the playground,'' she said, ''but we have one new student this year. His name is Dirk Engelman. He is originally from Ohio, but he and his parents have lived in England for the past year. Please make him feel at home in his new school.''

At recess the sixth grade boys chose up sides for a game of soccer. ''We get Scott for goalie,'' Jason yelled.

''Not fair,'' Matt answered. ''Then we'll never get a goal.''

Dirk stood on the sidelines, hands in his pockets, head thrown back, watching the game through narrowed eyes.

''Hey, Dirk,'' Jason finally shouted, ''want to play?''

Dirk shrugged. ''They play much better soccer in England. They'll probably switch me to a junior high team here.''

''Good!'' Scott muttered to Chris. ''Then we won't have to have him on our team.''

''I was the goalie on our championship team,''

Decisions

Dirk continued. He walked over and stepped in front of Scott. "Let me show you how," he said.

"Hey!" Matt ran up to Dirk. "You can't do that."

"Says who?" Dirk cocked his fists, ready to fight.

Just then the bell rang, and everyone ran to get in line. Dirk sauntered along behind the rest of the class, a slightly superior smile on his face.

When the bell rang for lunch, Mrs. Whitney asked Scott to stay in the room. "When you and your mother told me earlier about your diabetes, you said you'd bring some small cans of juice to keep here in case you have an insulin reaction. You get them, and I'll put them in my desk. You can ask for one when you need it."

Scott brought the cans of juice to Mrs. Whitney's desk. "Maybe I could keep them in my desk and then get one out if I need it," he suggested.

"No," she answered. "You can ask me if you need something, and I'll give it to you. I need to know if you're having a problem."

Scott nodded, but said to himself, *She's crazy if she thinks I'm going to interrupt class to ask for juice. And have everyone staring and laughing. No way!*

Scott hurried to get in the hot-lunch line. *Oh, yuck,* he said to himself when he picked up his tray.

Fruit cup! Maybe I can skip it, he thought. *I didn't get much exercise at recess.*

While Scott had been talking to Mrs. Whitney, most of the sixth graders had finished eating and gone out to the schoolyard. Scott hurried through his meal. *I'd better eat as much as I can,* he decided, *even if I'm not very hungry.* Just as he picked up his fork to finish his potatoes, Dirk sat down beside him.

"Hey," Dirk said. "Why don't you stay after school, and I'll show you how a really good goalie plays. Of course, once Coach Rollins sees how good I am, you won't have a chance."

That does it, Scott thought. He dropped his fork onto his plate, grabbed his tray, and jumped up from the table. He scraped his potatoes and fruit cup into the garbage and headed for the schoolyard.

Gym class was right after lunch, and then Mrs. Whitney spent the rest of the afternoon introducing the subjects the class would study during the year. Finally she announced that she would read to the class for the last fifteen minutes.

Scott had trouble concentrating on the story. He felt funny, almost dizzy. *I should've finished my lunch,* he thought. *I wish I had some juice in my desk.*

Scott shifted in his chair to look at the clock.

Even that small movement brought frowns from two classmates. Dirk stared at him from across the aisle. Everyone else was listening to the story. *I'll be all right until I get home—it's only ten minutes away,* Scott thought.

When the bell rang, he was the first one out the door. By the time he reached home, his hands were shaking. When he opened the garage door, he saw that his mother's car was gone. He'd forgotten that she had to work this afternoon. *Oh well,* he thought, *I'll just get the key off the hook in the cupboard.*

Scott found the key and tried to unlock the door. He couldn't get the key in the lock. Now he knew he needed to get inside and find some juice. The key wouldn't go in! He could feel tears running down his face. Everything was blurry, and he felt kind of dizzy.

Scott heard the garage door open. Melissa suddenly appeared beside him. ''Are you hurt?'' she asked. ''Why are you crying?'' He looked at her, but his tongue seemed to have quit working, and he couldn't answer.

''Oh, no!'' she exclaimed. ''You must be having one of those insulin reactions.'' Quickly she unlocked the door and led him to the kitchen.

''Sit down,'' she said, as she ran to the refrigerator. She handed Scott a glass of orange juice.

"Drink this—drink it right now," she said. She took his hand and pushed the glass toward his mouth.

Scott drank the juice, then closed his eyes. He felt very strange. He heard Melissa's voice, but it sounded very far away.

"Just rest a minute to let the sugar work," she said. "Then you'll need to have something to eat."

After awhile, Scott's head began to feel better. He opened his eyes. "I'm not dizzy now," he said, looking at Melissa's pale face. She looked scared, just like he felt.

"That was scary," she said.

Scott nodded. After eating half a sandwich, he felt fine again. "Did your reaction just start when you got to the house?"

"No," Scott answered. "It started at school."

"Next time you should drink some juice at school if you start feeling a reaction," Melissa said. "Don't you have juice there?"

"Yes," Scott said, "but Mrs. Whitney put it in her desk, so I have to ask her for it."

"I remember Mrs. Whitney," Melissa said. "She was strict, but she was a pretty good teacher."

"Well," Scott said, "I don't think I like her. Are the teachers in high school any better?"

Melissa laughed. "Not necessarily. My chemistry teacher's already piling on the homework. Why don't you rest," she suggested, "until Mom gets home from work."

Scott went to his room, lay on his bed for a few minutes, and then sat down at his desk to do his math homework. A short time later Mom knocked on his door.

"Melissa says you had a reaction after school," she said.

"Yeah—it was a really weird feeling," Scott said. "I was all shaky, and I couldn't do anything right." He hesitated, then added very quietly, "It was scary, too."

"I'll bet it was," Mom answered.

Scott looked up and saw tears in Mom's eyes. She leaned over and gave him a hug. "I know handling your diabetes isn't easy," she said. "But now you know that the next time you think your blood sugar is low at school, you should drink your juice before you come home."

"I know I should have," Scott answered, "but Mrs. Whitney put it in her desk, so I have to ask her for it."

"Well," Mom said, "she probably feels she should know if you're having any problems. She's responsible for you at school."

"But she was in the middle of reading," Scott

explained, "and everyone would've missed half the story if I'd raised my hand."

"So you were embarrassed to interrupt class?" Mom asked.

"I guess so." Scott shrugged. "Besides, then everyone would've started asking dumb questions."

"Maybe you can work out a compromise with Mrs. Whitney," Mom suggested. "She might let you keep the juice in a cupboard where you could go get it without asking. Then she would know when you got it, but you wouldn't have to interrupt the class. Would that help?"

"Yeah," Scott answered, "I suppose so." But to himself he said, *Nothing is going to help unless I can get rid of this stupid disease. I hate it!*

THREE
Field Trip

A couple of weeks later, Scott and Chris walked home from school together. "Tomorrow should be fun," Chris said. "I like field trips, and the hospital should be pretty interesting."

Not from the inside, Scott thought. Aloud, he said, "I'm not sure some of the girls think so. Matt told them his dad was going to take us into surgery so we could watch an operation. All that blood!''

During supper Mom mentioned the field trip. ''Even though you're supposed to be back before school is out, you need to take some food with you in case of a delay.''

''I'll have something in the bus,'' Scott answered.

''Okay,'' Mom said. ''I think Mrs. Whitney understands that you need to take a snack on field trips.''

''No problem,'' Scott insisted. ''I can handle it.''

''I know you can,'' Mom answered. ''But sometimes you act as if the diabetes will just go away if you ignore it long enough.''

Maybe it will, Scott thought. But aloud, he said, ''I'll be careful.''

When Scott and Chris arrived at school the next morning, the other sixth graders were talking about the field trip.

''My dad drove an ambulance in World War II in France,'' Dirk said, ''so I know all about emergencies. Maybe I'll be a doctor.''

Matt spoke up. ''It took my dad lots of years to go to medical school. I don't think I want to go to school that long.''

Suzy joined the group. ''Girls can be doctors,

too, you know. I'm going to be an internist like my Aunt Mary. She examines people and runs lab tests to find out what kind of problem they have. It's like figuring out a puzzle.''

I don't know, Scott thought to himself. *Then you'd have to tell someone they have something wrong, like diabetes. That part wouldn't be so great.*

The class was scheduled to go to the hospital right after gym class. Scott plopped into the seat beside Chris on the bus. ''Whew!'' he said. ''Mr. Jenkins really worked us today. He must think we all want to be track stars.''

When the bus arrived at the hospital, the students were met by Mr. Klein, the assistant administrator. ''One of the things you'll learn about today is the many different kinds of jobs that people in a hospital do,'' he said. ''You probably have a fairly good idea of what doctors and nurses do, but you may not be as familiar with the work of people such as dietitians or medical and X-ray technicians. A dietitian, for example, teaches people about food and oversees the kitchen and all the special meals that patients in the hospital need.''

Like people with diabetes, Scott thought.

A woman in a nurse's uniform stood beside Mr. Klein. ''I'm Mrs. Trotter,'' she said. ''I'll be your guide today.''

The class quickly toured the various departments. When they neared the pediatric department, Scott stayed in the back of the group. *I hope none of the nurses recognize me from this summer,* he thought.

Mrs. Trotter led the group into the nursery, where they could see the babies through the glass window, and then to the pediatric ward, where the patients were older children. ''Have any of you ever stayed overnight in a hospital?'' she asked.

Dirk spoke up. ''I had my appendix out three years ago,'' he said. ''It almost burst,'' he added proudly. ''I could've died.''

Scott started to raise his hand but quickly pulled it back. *What's wrong with me?* he thought. *If I say I've been in the hospital, everyone will want to know why.*

In the dietary department one of the dietitians explained some of the diets prescribed for people in the hospital. For example, some people aren't allowed salt, some people are on low-calorie diets, and, she said, ''people with diabetes have a special meal plan, also.''

''My grandmother has diabetes,'' Becky said. ''She takes pills, but I know a girl who has it, and she gives herself shots.''

''That's because there are two types of diabetes," Mrs. Trotter answered. "Your grandmother has type II diabetes. This type can usually be controlled by diet, exercise, and pills. Your girlfriend has type I diabetes. This type of diabetes is controlled with daily insulin injections, exercise, and diet."

Becky spoke up again. "My girlfriend has a little machine that she uses to check her blood. What does that have to do with diabetes?"

"First," Mrs. Trotter said, "let me explain diabetes very briefly. When you have type I diabetes, your pancreas quits making insulin. That's why your friend gives herself insulin injections every day. Some people take two injections a day, some take four, and some even take six. It all depends on their diabetes. The job insulin does in the body is to keep the level of the sugar in your blood normal. When you have diabetes, you need to check your blood sugar, so it won't get too high or too low."

Scott sighed. *Great,* he thought, *now I have to hear about diabetes on field trips, too.*

"But what about that machine she uses?" Becky asked.

"I'll get one and show you how it works." Mrs. Trotter was gone for a minute and returned with a blood-glucose monitor identical to Scott's.

When Mrs. Trotter pricked her finger to get a

drop of blood, several children groaned. No one moved or said a word while she demonstrated the use of the machine. When she finished, she showed them the digital readout on the small screen.

"Neat," Matt said. "How often do you have to do that if you have diabetes?"

"Most people with diabetes who do self-monitoring of blood glucose check their blood-sugar level three or four times a day," she answered.

"I couldn't do that," Jason said.

Mrs. Trotter smiled. "If you had diabetes, you'd need to learn how in order to keep your diabetes in good control."

"Well," Jason said, "what happens if you don't have good control?"

"You can have problems," Mrs. Trotter explained, "with either too little sugar or too much. High blood sugar usually develops more slowly than low blood sugar. A person with high blood sugar may be very thirsty, very tired, and have to urinate a lot. But sometimes," she said, "a person with high blood sugar may not be able to walk straight or talk properly. In this case, you have to act is if his or her blood-sugar level is low."

"Now," Mrs. Trotter continued, "if your blood sugar is too low, you can have an insulin reaction.

Whenever a person with diabetes seems very tired, or can't walk straight or talk properly, he or she probably has low blood sugar. If you have a friend with diabetes, you need to know how to treat an insulin reaction."

"What should you do?" Becky asked.

"You should give the person something with sugar in it as quickly as you can," Mrs. Trotter answered. "Regular soda pop, sugar cubes, or candy will work. It's very important to treat someone with low blood sugar as soon as possible, so remember to give your friend something with sugar in it."

That's what I need, Scott thought, *some sugar.* He felt sweaty but no one else looked uncomfortable. Scott turned away from the group and reached into his shirt pocket for a sugar tablet. *I'll eat a couple now,* he thought. *Then I can eat my snack on the bus.*

Jason spoke up. "How do you know if you have diabetes—I mean, how do you get it?"

"Well," Mrs. Trotter said, "doctors aren't sure what causes diabetes. But we do know that it's nothing the person does. And we know it's not contagious," she said. She turned to Becky and said, "That means you can't catch it from your girlfriend."

Then Mrs. Trotter looked back at Jason and

said, "You know you have diabetes when your doctor diagnoses it. But some of the symptoms for type I diabetes, which is the kind children and young adults get, are feeling tired, losing weight and being thirsty. And speaking of being thirsty," she said, leading them through another door, "we have lemonade and cookies for you here in the cafeteria. Help yourselves."

Scott stood by himself as most of the class continued to ask Mrs. Trotter questions. *I'm really hungry,* he thought. *I think I'll have lemonade since we had all that extra exercise in gym class.* He helped himself to lemonade and several cookies.

Mrs. Whitney came over to where Scott was standing. "Are you okay?" she asked. "You look a little pale."

Several kids turned and looked at Scott when they heard Mrs. Whitney.

"I'm okay!" Scott frowned. *Why can't she just leave me alone?* he thought.

She touched his shoulder lightly. "I just wanted to be sure you were all right," she said. She waited a moment, then turned and walked back to the front of the room.

Chris sat down beside Scott on the bus. "That was a good field trip!" he said. "You could have told them all that stuff about diabetes. Right?"

Field Trip

Scott didn't answer. *It just isn't fair,* he said to himself for at least the hundredth time. *It just isn't fair.*

FOUR

Out of Control

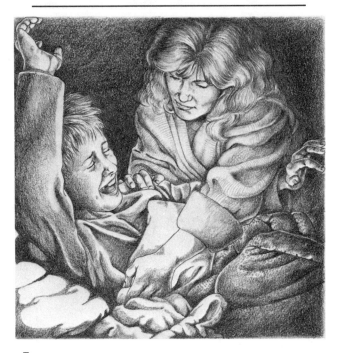

ater that night Scott was in his room doing homework when he heard the phone ring. Mom answered. "Oh," he heard her say. "Is something wrong, Mrs. Whitney?"

Scott went to the top of the stairs to listen, but Mom wasn't saying much.

Dad spoke up as soon as she hung up the telephone. "What was that all about?" he asked.

"That was Scott's teacher," Mom explained. "She said that Scott looked very pale at the hospital during the field trip, so she asked him if he was all right. She said he was rather rude and seemed to want to be left alone."

"Well," Dad said, "she's probably overreacting. Nothing happened, did it?"

"No," Mom admitted. "She just thought we'd want to know that he often looks tired or needs juice by the end of the afternoon. I'll check with Dr. Carrington tomorrow about adjusting Scott's morning insulin dosage or his meal plan."

"It seems to me as if Scott is handling everything just fine," Dad said. "She's being overprotective, just like you are most of the time." There was silence for a minute. Scott could picture Dad pulling at his beard like he always did during an argument.

"Maybe that's better than not caring at all," Mom answered.

"I care," Dad said. "It's just that I think you're suffocating Scott by constantly checking on him. He's twelve years old, and he's the one with diabetes, not you."

"That's not fair!" Mom's voice quivered. "I do worry too much, I suppose. But you couldn't even bother coming to the classes at the hospital. That leaves the whole burden on me. Even Melissa knows more about diabetes than you do."

"You know I couldn't leave work for an entire week to go to diabetes classes. Besides, Scott is doing just fine without you hanging over his shoulder every minute." Dad's footsteps sounded in the hallway. "I'm going for a walk," he said. The front door slammed behind him.

Scott went back to his room. He sat down at his desk and stared at his math homework.

Just then Melissa knocked on his door. "What's going on?" she asked. "I heard the front door slam."

"Dad slammed it when he left. He and Mom had a fight," Scott said.

"What were they fighting about?"

Scott shrugged, picked up his pencil, and pretended to work on his math.

"Oh, well," she said. "It was probably just some silly misunderstanding. They never stay mad for long."

After Melissa left, Scott sat and stared at his unfinished homework. *What did I do wrong to end up in this mess?* he asked himself. *Now Mom and Dad are mad at each other, and it's all my fault.*

A few minutes later, Scott went downstairs. He peeked into the family room, but no one was around.

"Is that you, Scott?" Mom was in the kitchen.

"Yes," he answered. "I'm going to check my blood sugar now." *Maybe if I stay in the bathroom long enough, she'll go upstairs,* he thought. *Then I won't have to answer dumb questions about Mrs. Whitney.*

Scott's blood sugar was 250, much higher than it should be. *I guess I'll just skip my snack tonight,* he decided. *Then I'll have a normal blood sugar in the morning.*

The light was off in the kitchen, so Scott knew Mom had already gone upstairs. He quietly returned to his room, where his math homework was still laying unfinished on the desk. He slammed the book shut and dropped it into his schoolbag. *Who cares!* he said to himself. *Mrs. Whitney can be mad at me, too. Everyone else is.*

After getting into bed and turning out his light, Scott lay staring at the ceiling for a long time. Finally he clenched his fists and squeezed his eyes shut tight. "Please, God," he whispered, "I'll even try to be friends with Dirk if you'll just make this diabetes go away." Then, with a loud sigh, he rolled over and went to sleep.

Suddenly he sat up in bed. *Something's after me!* he thought. He felt funny. There was a big hand trying to grab him. He tried to tell it to go away, but his tongue couldn't shape the words. He heard crying, though. Who was crying?

A voice was calling to him from the end of a tunnel. It was Mom's voice. "Scott," the voice said, "wake up."

The strange feeling began to fade away. Mom's voice sounded closer. "Scott," she said, "are you okay now?"

He looked around. It was still nighttime. Part of his room was dark, but the light on his bedside table was on. Mom and Dad were sitting on his bed, and Melissa was standing in the doorway.

Scott blinked and frowned. "What's going on?" he asked.

"You had an insulin reaction in your sleep," Mom said.

Scott rubbed his face. "Why is my face all sticky?"

"That's the liquid glucose I used to treat your reaction," Mom explained. "It's sticky because it's full of sugar. I squeezed it into your cheek from this bottle, but you kept spitting it out. I'll fix you a sandwich, so you can get back to sleep and not have this problem again tonight. We'll check your blood sugar, too."

"That was creepy," Scott said. "I thought this hand was after me, but it was my own hand."

"At first I thought you were having a nightmare from watching scary movies on TV," Mom said. "You were shaking and crying."

"Look," Scott said, holding out his hand. "I'm still shaking."

"I'm shaking a little myself," Mom said. "That must have been frightening for you."

Mom looked over at Dad. "You and Melissa can get some sleep," she said. "I'll make Scott a sandwich."

Scott sat at the kitchen table drinking a glass of milk while Mom fixed a grilled cheese sandwich. "That really was scary," he said. "It was like a nightmare, but I was awake, and it was still going on."

After eating his sandwich and checking his blood sugar, Scott followed Mom back upstairs. "I'm really tired," he said. "What time is it?"

"It's four o'clock in the morning," Mom said. "Not exactly the usual time for a grilled cheese sandwich." She sat down on Scott's bed. "I'll just sit here a few minutes until you get to sleep."

When Scott woke up again, sunlight shone through the drapes. *Why am I so tired?* he wondered. Then he remembered. He'd always figured that if he had an insulin reaction at night, he'd just sleep through it. This nightmare stuff was terrible.

Scott dragged himself out of bed and downstairs to the kitchen. "I'm really tired," he said.

Mom looked up from pouring milk. "You look tired," she said. "I called Dr. Carrington's office

33

and talked to his nurse. She suggested you stay home this morning, and she made an appointment for us to see Dr. Carrington at twelve-thirty.''

''I'll be glad to go back to bed.'' Scott rested his chin on his hands.

''Did you already do your injection?'' she asked.

''No,'' Scott shrugged. ''I forgot.'' When Mom made no reply, he looked up.

Finally, she said, ''I'll get the syringe ready for you, but you know it's important to remember.''

''I'm tired of remembering,'' Scott muttered. He started to roll up his sleeve.

''Aren't you supposed to be giving your injections in your legs this week?'' Mom asked.

''I guess so.'' Scott rolled down his sleeve, took the syringe, and gave himself the injection in his thigh.

''By the way, Scott,'' Mom said, ''what was your blood sugar before bedtime? You should eat more if it's low.''

''It wasn't low—it was too high,'' he said. ''It was 250, so I figured if I skipped my snack it would be back down to normal in the morning.''

''Well, it's true that adjustments can be made in your diet, but you should never skip your bedtime snack,'' Mom said. ''If you think you need to make adjustments in your meal plan, you and

I probably ought to talk about that with Dr. Carrington, or with the dietitian at the hospital. Why didn't you check with me about it?''

Scott suddenly began eating toast, so he wouldn't have to look at Mom. ''I didn't want to bother you,'' he said.

''You know I don't mind.'' There was a long pause. ''I suppose you heard Dad and me arguing, didn't you?''

Scott nodded.

Mom sat down at the table. ''I guess we're all having to make some adjustments. The reason we're seeing Dr. Carrington during the lunch hour is because your dad decided he wanted to be there, too.'' She reached over and laid her hand on Scott's shoulder. ''Don't worry about us arguing. It's not your fault that we don't always agree, even about how to treat diabetes.''

FIVE

Doctor

Carrington

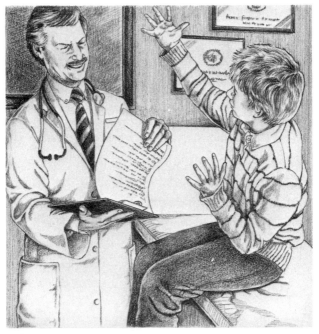

Scott spent the morning in bed, then shower-
ed and ate lunch.

"Ready to go?" Mom asked. Without waiting
for an answer, she said, "I suppose you're still
tired, aren't you?"

Scott nodded.

"Dr. Carrington can help you adjust your insulin or whatever needs to be done," she said.

Doctor Carrington

They met Dad at the doctor's office. Mrs. Mosely, Dr. Carrington's nurse, showed them into a room. She was short and plump and reminded Scott of his kindergarten teacher, who always used to hug the kids as they came into class.

She smiled at Mom and Dad and then turned to Scott. "Hello again," she said. "I'm going to weigh you and then check your temperature and blood pressure." As she finished the procedures, she looked up at Scott. "How do you like sixth grade?" she asked.

"It's okay," Scott said.

"And you're still playing soccer?"

Scott nodded.

"What position do you play?" she asked.

"I usually play goalie, but sometimes I substitute as a forward."

Mrs. Mosely turned to Mom and Dad. "Dr. Carrington likes young people who have diabetes to get involved in sports activities. Regular exercise really helps keep blood-sugar levels under control."

Dr. Carrington came in a few minutes later. He was a tall, thin man with stooped shoulders and brown eyes. He smiled and said hello to Mom and Dad, then turned to Scott.

"Hi Scott, how's school going?" he asked.

"All right," Scott said.

"And how have you been feeling?"

Scott shrugged. "Okay, I guess."

"Do you have any trouble with your injections?"

"Well, not really, except it takes too long to do them. And sometimes I forget."

"That happens to everyone," Dr. Carrington said. "You need to figure out a place to keep your insulin where you'll be reminded when you eat your meals."

Mom interrupted. "The day he forgot, we were eating sandwiches for supper and watching TV in the family room. His diabetes supplies are in a cupboard beside his chair in the kitchen."

Dr. Carrington looked through the record book that Scott kept of his blood sugars. "It looks as if you're doing a good job keeping track of your sugar levels," he said. But then he stopped. "Scott, could you tell me what happened here?" He was pointing to the day Scott had walked home from school while having an insulin reaction.

"Well, it was scary, but nothing like last night. I just didn't feel too hot. I guess walking home then wasn't such a good idea," Scott said.

"That's right," said Dr. Carrington. "You should always treat an insulin reaction immediately, no matter where you are. I imagine you'll remember that." Scott nodded.

Doctor Carrington

Mom spoke up again. "Scott's teacher at school thinks he often looks pale or seems tired late in the afternoon."

"Is that true, Scott?" Dr. Carrington asked.

"Sometimes," Scott said, "but not every day."

"Do you take your lunch or eat hot lunch?" Dr. Carrington asked.

"I eat hot lunch."

"Maybe you're not getting enough to eat on some days and then your blood sugar is low in the afternoon."

"I always get seconds if I think I need more," Scott said. "Besides, I bring the menus home, and Mom and I decide if I need to take something extra or skip part of the meal."

"That's a good idea," Dr. Carrington said. "So we need to look for something else that's causing the problem. Do you have gym every day?" he asked.

"No," Scott said.

"Maybe your blood sugar is low just on gym days."

Scott thought about that for a minute. "It might be," he said. "Gym is right after lunch, so if I remember that we have gym that day, I eat one or two extra breads. But I don't always think about it."

"Well," Dr. Carrington said, "your blood

sugar isn't consistently low late in the afternoon, but I think we ought to decrease your morning insulin somewhat. And I'd like you to try to remember to eat two extra breads on the days you have gym. Will you do that?''

"Yes," Scott answered. "I'll remember."

"Now," Dr. Carrington continued, "tell me about the insulin reaction you had last night."

"It was real scary, like a nightmare. I thought there was a big hand coming at me, but it was really just my own hand."

"Well, I'm sure it must have been very frightening for all of you," Dr. Carrington said.

"It sure was," said Dad.

"Yes, I was almost afraid to go back to sleep," Mom said.

"Scott, do you know why that happened?" Dr. Carrington asked.

"I skipped my bedtime snack because my blood sugar was 250," Scott said. "I knew that was too high, so I figured if I didn't eat, it would be back to normal this morning. Boy, was I wrong!"

Dr. Carrington smiled. "Well Scott, you're not alone—nighttime reactions happen to some people who have diabetes and take insulin," he said. "Did you get a lot of exercise yesterday?"

"Chris and I practiced soccer before supper

and then I rode my bike later," Scott said.

"You have to remember," Dr. Carrington explained, "that exercise doesn't necessarily lower your blood-sugar level right away. In fact, sometimes your blood sugar goes up after exercise and then drops later. That may have happened to you last night."

"Well, I won't skip my snack again!"

"Bedtime isn't a good time to be making that kind of adjustment," Dr. Carrington said. "You definitely need a bigger snack if your blood sugar is low, but correcting high blood sugars is something you should do the following morning by adjusting your insulin dose. As you become more familiar with your diabetes, we'll talk more about that," he added.

Dr. Carrington turned to Mom and Dad. "Do you keep glucagon on hand?" he asked.

"Yes," Mom said. "But I used the liquid glucose because one person in the classes at the hospital said he gets severe headaches from using glucagon. Also, Scott was still conscious enough to swallow."

"I don't like to sound stupid," Dad said, "but what is glucagon?"

"It's a hormone that is given by injection to treat hypoglycemia or low blood sugar like Scott had last night," Dr. Carrington explained. "What you did was fine, but you should keep the gluca-gon on hand,'' he said. ''Well Scott, if you have another nighttime reaction, we'll look into chang-ing your insulin regimen so that doesn't happen again,'' said Dr. Carrington. ''Do you have any other questions?'' he asked.

Mom hesitated. ''I worry about Scott giving the wrong insulin dosage. He's pretty sleepy some-times in the morning when he's preparing his in-jection.''

Dr. Carrington thought for a moment. ''Do you eat right after you get up, Scott? Or do you get ready for school first?''

''I usually eat first,'' Scott said.

''I often measure the insulin for him before breakfast,'' Mom said, ''because it bothers me to see him do it when he barely seems awake.''

''I really prefer that Scott do the whole proce-dure himself,'' Dr. Carrington said. ''Then he'll get used to it, and you won't need to worry if he stays overnight at a friend's or if you're out of town. Could you get ready for school first, so you'd be more awake, Scott?''

''I guess so,'' Scott said.

''Why don't you try it that way.'' Dr. Carring-ton looked over at Mom and Dad again. ''How's the family doing?'' he asked. ''Coping pretty well?''

Dad spoke up. "We don't always agree on how much supervision Scott needs," he said. He glanced at Mom. "I thought Elaine was being overly concerned about how much Scott ate, his insulin dosage, etc., but his insulin reaction last night made me realize that there's more to regulating diabetes than I thought."

"If Scott had just asked me about his snack last night," Mom said, "I would have told him not to skip it. Then everything would have been all right."

"Don't blame yourself," Dr. Carrington said. "Scott has to learn how to keep his diabetes in control. However," he said, glancing over at Scott, "he also should ask for advice when he's not sure. It's important for parents to find a balance between being overprotective and not providing any supervision at all. Education really is the key. The more you know, the better equipped you are to make choices."

"Well," Mom said, "I'll try to stop worrying so much and let Scott handle things on his own."

"I have one more suggestion," Dr. Carrington said. "It might be very helpful for you to meet and talk with other parents and children who are coping with diabetes, or to talk to one of the family counselors at the hospital. Scott's the one who has diabetes, but it affects the entire family. I'm going to give you a brochure about an excellent work-shop coming up in about three weeks that's for children with diabetes and their families. I think you should go to it.''

''We could probably do that,'' Mom said.

Dr. Carrington looked at Mom. ''Why don't you call me in about a week and let me know how Scott's doing. If he's not having any problems, I'd like to see him again in a month,'' Dr. Carrington said. ''At that time, I'll have the lab draw some blood and do a hemoglobin A_{1C} test. That will show us where Scott's blood-sugar level has been over the past one to two months. Please feel free to call me if you have any questions. And don't forget the workshop.''

On the way home, Mom was reading the brochure. ''I think it would be a good idea for all of us, including Melissa, to go to this workshop. It's in Fremont, and that's only about eighty miles away,'' she said.

''I can try to get away from work, but I can't promise anything,'' Dad said.

''It's on a Saturday,'' Mom said, ''and it's the same weekend as the state teachers' meeting, so Scott won't have a soccer game. I'll send in the registration tomorrow morning.''

That night Scott was lying in bed reading when he heard someone knock.

Dad poked his head around the edge of the door. ''May I come in?'' he asked.

Scott nodded. ''Did you just get home from your meeting?''

''Yes,'' Dad answered. ''And I wanted to see how you were feeling.''

''I feel fine now.'' Scott grinned. ''And I promise never to skip my bedtime snack again!''

''Good idea.'' Dad sat down on the edge of the bed. ''I really haven't been paying much attention to what diabetes is all about,'' he said. ''I just left everything up to you and your mother.''

''I know you're busy at work,'' Scott said.

''Yes, I am,'' Dad said. ''And I was using that as an excuse to let your mother do everything. Now I realize that if we're going to go fishing together, I need to know how to help with your diabetes.'' Dad leaned down and hugged Scott hard. ''You must still be tired from last night. Try to get a good night's sleep.''

SIX

Halloween Plans

"Hey, Scott!'' Chris caught up with his friend on the way home from school. It was two weeks before Halloween. ''What are you going to be for Halloween?'' he asked.

''Maybe I'll just forget Halloween this year,'' Scott said. ''I heard Dirk tell Suzy that costumes were just 'kid stuff.' Maybe he's right.''

Chris shrugged. ''Aw, don't listen to him. What

does he know?''

''Well,'' Scott said, ''I can't eat candy anyway, and that's what they'll have at school.''

''You mean because you have diabetes?'' Chris asked.

''Right,'' he answered. ''No candy!''

''You need a costume for the school party anyway,'' Chris said. ''We'll have the best haunted house that any sixth grade's ever had.''

''Well, I suppose that'll be fun. Maybe I'll be a monster or Dracula—something to really scare the girls,'' Scott said.

''Neat idea,'' Chris agreed. ''Why don't you come over, and we'll work on costumes? My mom has all kinds of old clothes.''

''I have to go home first and eat my snack. Then I'll come over.''

''You know,'' Chris said, ''I know it's no fun having diabetes, but it must be nice to have a snack after school every day. My mom always says it'll ruin my supper.''

''But I'm not hungry now,'' Scott protested, ''and I have to eat a snack anyway. And then, when I am hungry, I'm not supposed to eat. It's no fun.''

''My mom keeps telling me that you'll probably be healthier than all the rest of us because people with diabetes eat well-balanced meals.'' Chris laughed. ''I think she's going on a nutrition kick.''

"Mom tells me I'll probably have fewer cavities because I'm not eating all that sugar. I'd rather take my chances with the candy."

"Can't you ever have candy again?" Chris asked.

"Maybe once in awhile for a special treat or if my blood sugar is low."

Scott and Mom discussed Halloween while he ate his snack. "I want to be something scary," he explained, "because the sixth grade always has a haunted house for the school party. Mrs. Whitney put Chris and me in charge of setting it up. Say, do you think I could use that wooden ax that Melissa used in the play? Maybe I can be something scary with that."

"The ax is in the attic. You can get it if you want," Mom said.

When he got to Chris's house, Scott showed him the ax. "But," he said, "I can't think of any kind of monster that carries an ax."

Chris thought for a few minutes. "I've got it," he said at last. "You can be an executioner—you know, one of those guys that used to chop off people's heads with an ax. There's a picture of one in an old history book of my dad's. You can wear a black hood and a cape."

"That sounds neat. I knew you'd think of something. What are you going to be?" Scott asked.

Halloween Plans

"Well," Chris said, "if I'm Dracula, then I'd have a black cape, too. We can work on making them together. My mom made herself a black dress last winter and had a bunch of material left over. You could use that for your hood and cape. I think you could have a short cape, but Dracula needs a long one."

"I've got it!" Scott exclaimed. "For the seventh-grade play, Melissa dyed an old sheet black and used it for a backdrop. We could make that into a cape."

"Yeah, that'll work," Chris agreed. "We'll probably have to get some help with the sewing. I think my mom can help. Is your mom too busy at work?"

"Probably not," Scott answered. "They hired another person, so she's not working as many hours. I'm sure she can help. Let's find your mom's leftover material and then we can go find the black sheet."

While the boys dug out the materials they need-ed, Scott remembered something else. "Hey," he said, "we should look through my dad's records to see if he has any scary sounding music to use in the haunted house."

"I like that idea." Chris thought for a moment. "We can turn off all the lights in the sixth-grade room and have just a flashlight for light. I think we'll have to put blankets over the windows so it'll be dark enough.''

''We can get Matt and Jason to bring blankets,'' Scott said.

At supper that night, Scott asked Mom if she could help sew his costume.

''Yes,'' she said. ''That's no problem.''

''Would you fix some popcorn for the school party, too?'' he asked. ''Then there'd be at least one thing I can eat.''

''I can fix popcorn,'' Mom said. ''But maybe we should call Mrs. Benson, the dietitian at the hospital. She probably has some recipes for snacks that you could eat that everyone would like.''

''It has to be something good,'' Scott said.

''Maybe I'll call her,'' Mom said. ''I think I'll stop at the library, too. Mrs. Benson said they have some cookbooks with recipes especially for people with diabetes.''

''I had another idea, too,'' Scott said. ''Could I have a party here Halloween night?''

''I don't know,'' Mom said. ''You have quite a bit of work with a costume and the haunted house at school. What kind of a party did you have in mind?''

''I just wanted to have the guys on the soccer team come over and watch scary movies. No dumb party games or anything. We could just have popcorn and peanuts.''

''Well,'' Mom said, ''that sounds pretty easy. I think your dad would be willing to rent a video machine and some movies for one night.''

Scott went to his room with his head full of Halloween plans. *Tomorrow after soccer,* he thought, *I'll invite everyone to the party. Maybe I'll even invite Dirk.*

SEVEN
The Jets

T he next Saturday, the Eagles were scheduled to play the Jets, the only other unbeaten team in the soccer league. Scott woke up early to a cool, crisp breeze. It was a good day for a game.

At breakfast Mom seemed worried. "You know, Scott," she said, "your soccer game is right before lunch. You'll probably need an extra snack before or during the game, and I can't be there until the game is almost over.''

''I can handle it, Mom,'' Scott protested. ''I'm not a baby. I'll take a can of juice and some crackers with me and put them with my jacket.''

''Okay, I guess that's all right,'' she agreed. ''You know, I'd probably worry less if I could explain to some of the other parents what to do in case of an insulin reaction.''

Scott scowled. ''I don't want anyone to know,'' he insisted. ''Besides, the coach knows. That's enough.''

Mom sighed. ''All right,'' she agreed. ''I'll do it your way for now. But I hope you change your mind before you need some help sometime. You could at least wear the Medic Alert necklace that tells that you have diabetes.''

''I can't wear it while I'm playing. It won't stay inside my shirt, and it's always hitting me in the face. I said I'd take my juice. Chris can always get it for me if I get tired.''

''Well, I guess it's okay, because Coach Rollins knows you have diabetes,'' Mom said. ''But Scott, you have to remember that you're not always going to be around people who know that. I hope you have a good game. I'll try to get there before it's over.''

Mom dropped Scott at the soccer field and went on to work.

When everyone on the team had arrived, the coach called them together. ''The Jets are the only other unbeaten team in the league,'' he said. ''Let's try and keep our record going. Get out there and play your best.''

He assigned positions for the game. ''Dirk,'' he said, ''I'll start you off as goalie. For the second half, Scott will play.''

As the boys ran onto the field, the coach yelled, ''All right boys, get out there and play your best!''

Halfway through the first half, Matt, the Eagles's best forward, was kicked as he went after the ball. Coach Rollins motioned to Scott. ''I want Matt to sit out for a few minutes,'' he said. ''You play forward for the rest of this half.'' The score was zero to zero.

Oh boy, Scott thought, *this is my chance. Maybe I can make a goal.* But the Jets kept the ball and would have scored twice except that Dirk caught the ball both times and kicked it away.

As the team came off the field at halftime, Dirk punched Scott on the arm. ''Let's see you do that good a job as goalie,'' he jeered.

''No problem,'' Scott answered. ''I'll do all right.'' To himself he added, *I hope.*

Scott was tired from playing the extra time as forward, so he grabbed his jacket to get his can of juice. It was gone. He looked around and saw the can laying in the grass—empty! The crackers were missing, too. Just then he noticed Dirk watching him. *That Dirk,* he thought. *I'll bet he drank my juice.*

Dirk sauntered up. "What's wrong, little boy?" he asked. "You need your morning juice? I know babies always need to have an extra snack." He walked away laughing.

Scott clenched his fists. *Just you wait, Dirk,* he said to himself. *One of these days.* . . He left the thought unfinished.

Scott dropped his jacket when he heard Coach Rollins calling for the team to begin the second half. *No problem,* Scott decided. *I'm probably just tired from playing soccer, not because my blood sugar is low.* He grabbed the goalie's jersey and pulled it on as he ran out to the goal.

Both teams were getting tired, but the Jets still kept possession of the ball most of the time. Neither team had scored so far.

Scott concentrated on the ball. There was a long pass from the Jets, but he caught it and kicked it to one of his forwards. The Eagles took the ball down the field but failed to score. One minute left in the game and still no score. The Jets were coming down the field again.

Scott crouched, ready to pounce on the ball. It came right at him. He started forward to stop it, but his legs wouldn't move. He fell toward the ball, but it rolled by and into the goal. He heard the Jets cheering as he hit the ground. His teammates turned away and walked slowly back to the sideline. The whistle blew to signal the end of the game—their first defeat.

Scott couldn't get up. He lay in the grass, his head feeling very light. *I need some juice,* he thought, but getting up was too much effort.

Then he heard Mom's voice. ''Scott,'' she demanded. ''Sit up! I have some juice for you.'' She poured some into his mouth. He sputtered but managed to swallow some. He finished the juice and then ate a small bag of pretzels Mom kept in her purse.

''I'm all right now,'' he said. ''The team is going for pizza. I want to go along.''

''Well, I don't know.'' Mom sounded doubtful.

''I'm fine now. Please, Mom?''

''Well, all right,'' she finally agreed. ''By the way, I thought you said you were bringing juice to the game.''

''I did,'' Scott said. ''But someone drank it. I think it was Dirk. He doesn't like me because I'm just as good a goalie as he is. He thinks he should get to play more because he played in England.''

''I'm sorry you don't get along with him. Maybe he's just having trouble being the new boy, so he thinks he has to show off.''

''Maybe,'' Scott said. ''But I've tried being nice to him, and it doesn't help.''

Scott looked up and saw Coach Rollins walking toward them. ''Are you all right?'' he asked.

Scott nodded. ''I'm fine.''

''He had an insulin reaction,'' Mom said. ''He brought juice and crackers with him, but someone took them.''

''I'm sorry that happened,'' the coach said to Scott. ''Maybe next time you should leave your food with me.'' He turned to Mom. ''Can Scott still go with us for pizza?''

''Yes,'' she said. ''He's okay now, and the pizza will be fine for lunch.''

Scott ran to catch up with Chris as the team headed for Coach Rollins's van. ''What happened?'' asked Chris. ''Did you have one of those reactions?''

''Yes,'' Scott answered, ''but don't tell anyone.''

''Why not?'' Chris looked puzzled. ''If you don't tell anyone, they'll think you weren't trying hard enough.''

''Then they'll just have to think that.'' Scott gritted his teeth. ''Don't you dare tell!''

''I can keep a secret,'' Chris said. ''I won't tell if you don't want me to.''

Scott sighed. ''I just don't want anyone to know I have this weird disease. Okay?''

''The guys would understand,'' Chris persisted.

''Would you tell if you had it?'' Scott asked.

Chris hesitated. ''Maybe not,'' he admitted.

As they climbed into the van, Dirk looked up and laughed. ''Hey,'' he said, ''here comes the greatest goalie the Eagles ever had. If Coach Rollins had let me play the last quarter, we wouldn't have lost the game.''

''If you hadn't drunk my juice, we wouldn't have lost the game with me as goalie,'' Scott said.

Dirk looked surprised. ''What does that have to do with it?''

There was a long silence. Suddenly, Scott blurted out, ''Because I have diabetes, and I needed that juice.'' His voice shook very slightly. He turned away and pressed his forehead against the window. *Now I've done it,* he thought. *I should have gone home.*

Jason spoke up. ''What really happened, Scott?''

Chris looked over at Scott. No one said anything. ''Are you guys deaf?'' he asked. ''Scott said he has diabetes.''

''Says who?'' Matt demanded. ''He just made that up.''

Chris nudged Scott. ''C'mon, tell them.''

58

Scott looked up. ''I lost the game because my blood sugar was low, and someone took the juice and crackers I was supposed to eat.'' He glared at Dirk.

''If that's really true, why didn't you tell us before?'' Jason asked.

Scott shrugged. ''I thought you'd think I was a wimp or something.''

''Do you give shots and check your blood just like the nurse was showing us at the hospital?'' Jason asked.

''Yes,'' Scott answered.

''Wow!'' Jason said. ''You're not a wimp if you can do that.''

''I don't believe it,'' Matt said.

''It's true,'' Chris said. ''I've seen his syringes and blood-sugar testing machine.''

Just then the coach climbed into the van.

''Hey, Coach,'' Matt yelled. ''Did you know Scott has diabetes?''

''Yes,'' the coach said. ''I know that.''

Matt looked at Scott. ''It's really true!''

''Of course it is,'' Chris said. ''Nobody's going to make that up.''

When the team arrived at the pizza parlor, Chris sat down beside Scott. ''I'm glad you told about your diabetes,'' he said. ''Everybody thinks you're really neat to do all that stuff.''

And I was so worried, Scott thought. *Boy, was I dumb.*

Chris finished lunch first. "Are you ready to go to the arcade?" he asked.

"Go ahead," Scott said. "I'm going to have one more slice of pizza."

After Chris left, Dirk sat down. He cleared his throat. "I'm sorry I took your juice," he said. "I didn't know it was important."

Scott slowly finished eating. "Why don't you like me?" he finally asked.

Dirk shrugged. "I don't know," he said. "I guess I wanted everyone to like me, and they liked you instead." He hesitated. "Can you keep a secret?" he asked.

"Are you kidding? I kept my diabetes a secret for almost three months, didn't I?"

Dirk laughed. "That's true," he said.

"So what's the secret?" Scott was curious.

"Well," Dirk said. "I'm really supposed to be in junior high this year, but my folks moved around so much that I'm behind and had to take sixth grade over. I guess I was just mad about that. It doesn't seem fair."

"Just like me and diabetes," Scott said. "That doesn't seem fair, either."

"Friends?" Dirk asked.

Scott smiled. "Friends!" he answered.

EIGHT

Here to Stay

The day of the diabetes workshop, Scott's alarm woke him at six-thirty. "Oh no," he groaned.

He heard Melissa's voice downstairs. "Whose idea was this, anyway!" she said.

Mom laughed. "You'll live," she said. "Just get dressed, and we'll eat in the car."

They arrived in Fremont by eight-thirty and

found the hotel where the workshop was being held. After registering, they joined the other parents and children in a large conference room. Dr. Stewart from Fremont gave the opening lecture on ''The Family and the Child with Diabetes.''

After the lecture, the parents met in another conference room. The young people were divided into small groups, each one with a leader.

The leader for Scott and Melissa's group was named Jim. ''I'm twenty-two years old,'' he told them, ''and I've had diabetes since I was nine. I'd like each of you to tell the group your name and how long you've had diabetes.''

After the introductions, Jim looked around. ''The reason for these small groups,'' he said, ''is to give you a chance to talk about some of the things Dr. Stewart mentioned in his lecture. Do any of you have a subject to bring up?''

No one answered.

''Okay,'' he said, ''since food plays a big part in controlling diabetes, do any of you have any comments or complaints about following your meal plan?''

Brenda, who was fourteen, raised her hand. She was a slim girl with long black hair. ''I hate it when the rest of the family gets dessert, and I don't,'' she said. ''Mom serves chocolate cake and ice cream to everyone else, and I'm supposed to eat sliced peaches! If I can't have dessert, nobody should.''

''But that's not fair,'' said Sam, Brenda's younger brother. ''Why should I have to give up desserts? I don't have diabetes.''

Bill, who had red hair and freckles and was also fourteen, spoke up. ''I've had diabetes for six years,'' he said, ''and it still bothers me when people eat desserts that I can't have. I complained so much that Mom quit baking. Now they all just pig out when I'm gone.''

''What about you, Scott?'' Jim asked. ''You've only had diabetes a few months. What does your family do?''

Scott hesitated for a minute. ''My mom makes the rest of the family eat what I eat. She says it's healthier.''

''Boy, are you lucky,'' Brenda said.

Jim looked over at Melissa. ''Do you resent having to change your eating habits even though you're not the one with diabetes?''

Melissa thought for a minute. ''I guess I thought having diabetes was pretty tough on Scott,'' she said, ''so I didn't mind too much. Besides, Scott's the only one who has to eat certain amounts of everything. The rest of us just gave up desserts.''

Scott laughed. ''Except when she pigs out on

candy bars at the movies.''

"Well," Melissa said, "that's better than eating in front of you.''

Scott shrugged. "I suppose so.''

"My mom started making desserts with sugar substitutes," said Janey, a short, blond girl about Melissa's age. "They're pretty good.''

"C'mon," Sam said. "They're only good if you can't have the real thing. Right?''

"My mom made an apple pie with one of those substitutes," Bill said, "and it was okay.''

"Let's get back to Brenda and Sam," Jim said. "Brenda doesn't like it when her family eats desserts that she can't have, but Sam doesn't see why he should have to give up the things he likes even though he doesn't have diabetes. Sam, how do you think your family can solve the problem?''

"Well," Sam said, "I guess we could have dessert when she's not around. I could eat three chocolate cakes while she's talking to Fr-r-ed on the phone.''

Everyone laughed. Jim turned to Brenda. "Would that help?" he asked.

"I guess so," she said. "And I'll ask Mom to try the sugar substitutes. My dad needs to lose weight anyway.''

Janey laughed. "That's one of the best things about diabetes camp," she said. "Everyone eats the same food.''

''What's camp like?'' Scott asked.

''It's just like any other camp except everybody has diabetes,'' Janey answered. ''I've gone every year for seven years. Next summer I want to be a counselor.''

''You mean the counselors have diabetes, too?'' Scott asked.

''Sure,'' Janey answered. ''And there's a doctor and a nurse there all the time, so your parents don't have to worry. They can go home and eat chocolate cake every day!''

''We only have a few minutes left for this session,'' Jim said. ''Since Janey's had diabetes for almost eight years, I'm going to ask her if she has any advice for those of you who are more recently diagnosed.''

Janey thought for a minute. ''I guess I'd just say that having diabetes makes you grow up faster than other kids your age. It's hard when you have restrictions that none of your friends have. But if you don't take care of yourself, you'll be sorry later, because it's never going to go away. . .unless someone finds a cure.''

Her words seemed to echo in Scott's head. *It's never going to go away,* he thought. *I'm stuck with it.*

''Thanks, Janey,'' Jim said. ''Since we've been

talking about food, everyone's probably hungry, and it's time for lunch."

Following lunch, all the parents and children met again in the main conference room for a short film. Then Dr. Stewart stood up. "We're going to finish our workshop with a panel discussion on how families learn to cope with diabetes," he explained. "I'm going to ask each panel member to briefly introduce himself or herself."

Bill and Brenda and each of their mothers were on the panel. Brenda was the last one to introduce herself. "I'm fourteen," she said, "and I've had diabetes for almost a year. At first I thought my life was totally ruined." She paused. Then, with a slight shrug of her shoulders, she said, "And sometimes, I still think so!"

There was silence in the room. "I think everyone here can understand that," Dr. Stewart said. "What do you do when you start feeling that way?"

"Well," Brenda said, "sometimes I talk to my friends, and they're pretty sympathetic. That helps."

Bill spoke up. "It seems when you're really feeling down about having diabetes, that's just when your mother starts nagging you about checking your blood sugar." He looked over at his mom and grinned. "Sorry, Mom!" he said.

Here to Stay

His mother smiled. "I really try hard to keep quiet and not keep checking on Bill," she said. "He's had diabetes for six years and is old enough to take care of himself. But it's very hard not to ask about his blood sugars."

"I see a lot of you parents nodding your heads," Dr. Stewart said. "Interference from parents is a very common complaint among young people, starting about the time they reach junior high. Does anyone have any suggestions?"

Brenda's mother spoke up. "I have Brenda see her doctor regularly because she seems to take suggestions from him better than from me."

"That's an excellent idea," Dr. Stewart said. "It's also good for young people with diabetes to get in the habit of working with their doctor, nurse, dietitian, and social worker directly, instead of having the information always come from parents."

Bill's mother spoke up again. "But you can't just stand by and allow the diabetes to get out of control. That's not healthy."

"It's very hard to let go," Dr. Stewart agreed. "But young people have to make a decision about diabetes control, just as they have to make decisions about drinking and using drugs."

"Are you saying never to ask about blood-sugar levels and meal plans?" Bill's mother asked.

"No," Dr. Stewart said. "I think each family has to figure out what works best for them. Ask your sons or daughters how much they want you to check on them, but also let them know what worries you about diabetes control. Then figure out a system together that will satisfy everyone."

The workshop was over at four o'clock. "Maybe we'll see you here again next year," Janey said to Scott and Melissa. "And Scott, maybe I'll see you at camp next summer."

On the way home, Mom turned to the rest of the family. "I learned a lot today," she said. "How about the rest of you?"

"It was interesting to talk to other parents," Dad said. "I guess I've had my head in the sand. I need to be a little more aware of what's going on with Scott and his diabetes."

"And I found out that it's all right for me to let Scott do what he's supposed to without being constantly on his back," Mom said.

Melissa spoke up from the back seat. "Listening to those other kids made me realize how hard it is to have diabetes."

"It is hard," Mom said. "And sometimes we don't give Scott credit for how well he's doing. How about you, Scott?" she asked. "Are you glad you went?"

"Yeah—it was neat to talk to other kids that have

diabetes,'' Scott said. ''Can I go to diabetes camp next summer?''

''I think that's a good idea,'' Mom said. ''The parents we talked to said it was a good camp, and that the kids really like it.''

''That music camp I told you about isn't too far from the diabetes camp,'' Melissa said.

''Maybe you can both be at camp the same week,'' Mom said. ''We'll have to check the dates.''

Scott felt good when he went to bed that night. *That was neat,* he thought. *Mom and Dad aren't mad anymore. And maybe I can manage this dumb disease after all.*

NINE
The Haunted
House

On the day of the school Halloween party, Mom drove Chris and Scott to school with their costumes and supplies for the haunted house.

Right after lunch the sixth graders started setting up. Several of the boys covered the windows with blankets, and the girls set out treats to give to anyone brave enough to walk through the door.

''Those of you scheduled to help with games

for the first hour should go to the gym now,'' Mrs. Whitney said. ''Then you can switch places with the people here for the second hour.'' About half the class headed for the gym.

The rest of the sixth graders began putting costumes on over their clothes. Chris was dressed almost all in black—cape, pants, mask, and gloves. And attached to one glove was a furry black bat.

''Hey, where'd you get that bat?'' Scott asked. ''It looks pretty real.''

''My mom made it out of the same material we used to make your cape. Look, I can make it swoop down at the kids.'' Chris demonstrated by swinging his arm over his head and then down.

''If that doesn't scare 'em, nothing will,'' Scott said. ''I brought some spooky music we can play.''

''You need one or two people to run the record player,'' Mrs. Whitney said.

Suzy spoke up. ''Denise and I'll do that.''

''Everyone wearing a scary costume can stand by the table and take turns handing out the treats,'' Jason said. ''Let's put the table in the middle of the room, so everyone has to walk in to get a treat.''

''Good idea,'' Chris said. ''When they get close to the table, I'll make the bat swoop down at them.''

"I'll stand right inside the door," Scott said. "Should I say something or just stand there?"

"Stand real still until they get close," Matt suggested. "Then lower the ax and say, 'Are you ready to enter?' in a real deep voice."

"That's good," Chris said.

Scott looked around the room. "Where's Becky? She said she'd bring flashlights."

One of the girls dressed as a witch spoke up. "I've got them right here," Becky said, handing Scott the flashlights.

"I have an idea," Matt said. "I can hide behind a desk and shine one of the flashlights on Scott, and someone else can shine one on the people by the table. Then they won't see the rest of us at all."

"I'll hold the other flashlight," Jason said.

"We're about ready," Chris said. "Somebody turn out the lights."

"Got it!" Jason flipped the light switch.

"Not bad," Matt said. "This might actually scare someone."

"I'll be the lookout," Dirk said. "Then you'll know when someone's coming, but they won't see you." Dirk stuck his head around the edge of the door. "Two first graders are on the way," he said.

Everyone scrambled to get in place. Suzy started the music.

"Nobody move," Chris whispered. "Sh-h-h!"

The Haunted House

Two small boys hurried down the hallway, one dressed as a clown, the other as a cowboy. They stopped when they saw Scott.

Scott recognized the cowboy. He was six, and his name was Lucas. He always wanted to play with the older boys.

"Is that real?" Lucas asked.

The clown shook his head and took a step backward. "I dunno, but it looks scary," he said.

"Come on," Lucas said, pulling out one of his guns. "I'm not scared." He marched up to the door with the clown right behind him.

As they entered the room, Scott lowered the ax in front of them and said in as scary a voice as he could, "Are you ready to enter the haunted house?"

"I'm not scared!" Lucas said, scowling.

"You may enter," Scott said, lifting the ax.

The two boys peered inside. The room was dark except for the table, where the flashlight shone on the group of witches, monsters, and ghosts. Chris motioned for them to come in. The bat wings fluttered with the movement of his hand.

"I'm not scared." Lucas's voice shook a little as he watched the bat. He looked up at Scott standing right beside him.

Scott looked down through the eyeholes in his hood and saw Lucas's lower lip start to tremble.

Then a single tear ran down his freckled cheek.

Scott pulled up his hood. "Hey, Lucas—it's just me, Scott. That's Chris with the bat. You go on in and get a treat, okay?"

Lucas looked up and smiled a rather wobbly smile.

"Okay." His eyes looked about twice their normal size. The two boys ran inside, grabbed a treat and ran out again. "Hey," Lucas shouted as he ran down the hallway. "Look what we got. And I wasn't scared at all."

Scott turned around and then doubled over with laughter. "Did you hear that? Lucas wasn't scared at all."

The rest of the sixth graders burst into laughter. "It's a good thing you showed him who you were," Chris said. "He was going to cry."

Scott shrugged. "We don't want to give any little kids nightmares."

Dirk looked out the door. "Here come some fourth-grade girls. Get ready."

The three girls hesitated when they saw Scott standing perfectly still inside the door.

This is fun, Scott thought. *They don't know what to think.*

The girls approached cautiously. When Scott lowered his ax, one of them jumped.

"Halt!" he said. "Enter at your own risk."

The Haunted House

"Oh, I know that voice," said the girl dressed as Raggedy Ann. "You're on the soccer team." She looked inside the door. "And so's he," she said, pointing at Chris.

All three went through the door cautiously. "You don't scare us," Raggedy Ann announced loudly. They each grabbed a treat and hurried out the door. "That is pretty scary," Raggedy Ann admitted. "At least for little kids—but not for us." The girls giggled and hurried on down the hallway.

At the end of the hour, the sixth graders who had been helping in the gym came back to the haunted house.

"I'll leave my costume here for someone else to use," Scott told Mrs. Whitney. "I won't need it in the gym."

"I'll leave my cape and the bat here, too," Chris said. "We'll go help with the games."

"And eat," Scott said.

Scott and Chris spent the last hour in the gym helping with some of the games and eating popcorn.

When school was over, Mom was waiting to drive them home.

"Mom," Scott asked, "did you tell Mrs. Balzor that I have diabetes?"

"No," Mom answered, "but she may have

heard about it from Mrs. Whitney. Probably most of the teachers know.''

Scott shrugged. ''Well, she knew somehow. Everybody got a little sack of candy when they left school, and she fixed a special one for me. It has sugarfree gum and a little bag of pretzels. And Mrs. Whitney bought me a can of sugarfree pop from the machine in the teachers' lounge.''

''That was very nice,'' Mom said.

''Yeah,'' Scott said. ''I didn't like her at first, but I guess she's okay.''

That night the soccer team came over and watched two horror movies. Chris was the last one to leave. ''This was a really neat Halloween,'' he said.

''Yeah, it was fun,'' Scott agreed.

When he went to bed, Scott had trouble falling asleep. *I didn't think Halloween would be any fun at all this year,* he thought, *and we had a great time.*

TEN
Jamboree

S cott leaped out of bed on the Saturday morning following Halloween. He looked out the
window and heaved a sigh of relief. It looked like
perfect weather for the Soccer Jamboree. The first
game was at nine-thirty. Scott dressed quickly and
ran downstairs to eat breakfast.

Mom was setting the table for breakfast. ''I'm
really sorry that none of us can be at the Jamboree.

Dad has a meeting, I have to help with inventory at the store, and Melissa has cheerleading practice. One of us will at least get there to pick you up after lunch.''

Scott was busy measuring the insulin for his injection. ''That's okay, Mom. I'll eat an extra piece of toast for breakfast. Besides, almost everyone on the team said he's bringing juice for me.''

Mom sat down to drink her coffee. ''Well,'' she said, ''you should go ahead and take what you need yourself.''

''Okay,'' Scott agreed. ''I have cans of juice and a sandwich in my schoolbag, in case I need anything before lunch.''

''Are you taking your glucose monitor with you?'' Mom asked.

''Yes,'' Scott said. ''And I'll give everything to the coach.''

Mom smiled. ''I just wish I could be there.''

''I'll be okay. We can have as many hot dogs as we want at lunch. Besides, you're supposed to stop worrying. Remember?''

''Okay,'' she said. ''I'll be quiet. If I have to worry, I'll try not to do it out loud.''

When Scott arrived at the soccer field, he began practicing with a few other early arrivals. Then Coach Rollins and the rest of the team showed up, and practice began in earnest.

Jamboree

"We'll be playing four thirty-minute games before lunchtime," Coach Rollins explained. "We're eight and one in the regular season, so let's see if we can keep up the good work."

The morning passed quickly, with the Eagles winning every game by at least two goals. But their last game was against the Jets, the only team that beat them during the regular season.

During the fifteen-minute break between games, Scott grabbed his schoolbag and sat down by the fence with Chris. He leaned back and closed his eyes. "I'm pooped!"

Chris grabbed his shoulder. "You can't be tired now. We need you if we're going to beat the Jets."

Scott sat up and reached for his schoolbag. "I'll check my blood sugar and see if I need a snack." Scott did the test as several team members gathered around to watch.

"What now?" Jason asked.

Scott laughed as he pulled half a peanut-butter sandwich from his schoolbag. "I'll have my snack, and then we'll beat the Jets."

The game started with both teams playing hard. Scott played forward and made a goal in the first half, but the Jets matched the Eagles goal for goal. At the end of the first half, Coach Rollins told Scott to play goalie.

Oh no, Scott said to himself. *If they score against*

me, everyone will blame me for losing the game—just like last time.

Scott grabbed the goalie's jersey and headed onto the field. He turned around when he heard his name called.

It was Dirk. "You can do it!" he yelled.

The whistle blew and the second half started. The Eagles had the ball but lost it. The Jets took it down the field but were called for a foul, and the Eagles had the ball again. Still they were unable to score. Finally, after several tries, Chris shot a goal, and the Eagles were ahead 5-4 with two minutes left to play.

The Jets put their best forward back into the game. He took the ball and dribbled down the field, weaving around the Eagle players and closing in on the goal.

Scott watched the players coming down the field. *Okay,* he said to himself, *don't take your eyes off the ball. Watch it every second.*

The Eagles fullbacks were trying to take the ball away, but the Jets kept moving toward the goal.

"Eyes on the ball," Scott whispered. "Eyes on the ball."

The forward for the Jets swerved to the right and kicked the ball hard, straight toward the goal.

Scott made a dive for the ball. *Oh no,* he

thought, *I'm going to miss it.* He stretched out his arms and felt the ball touch his fingertips. As his knees hit the ground, he scrambled forward, grabbed the ball, and fell on it. The team cheered as the whistle blew. The Eagles had won!

Coach Rollins clapped Scott on the shoulder. "Great save, Scott! You've become an excellent goalie. And I knew you wouldn't let diabetes stop you from doing what you wanted."

Scott smiled. "Let's eat," he said. "I'm hungry." The team raced to the school gym for hot dogs and pop.

While the boys were eating, Coach Rollins walked up. "Our turn for team pictures," he announced. The Eagles lined up at the front of the gym where each team was having its picture taken.

"The awards ceremony will be next," the coach said, "so don't leave after the picture."

A few minutes later, Mr. Peterson, one of the junior high coaches, asked everyone to be quiet.

"We're going to give out the awards and trophies," he said. Winners were announced for each grade level, and a traveling trophy was presented for display at the winning team's school.

The sixth-grade trophies were last. "We have two excellent teams in this age category," Mr. Peterson said. "The Jets were unbeaten in the regular season, and the Eagles lost only one game. However, the Eagles were unbeaten in the Jamboree. Because of these outstanding records, the committee has decided to award each of these teams a first-place trophy.'' Everyone applauded. ''Will a player from each team please come forward to accept the trophy?''

Coach Rollins looked around. ''Who's going to go up?'' he asked.

''Scott should be the one,'' Dirk said.

Scott stepped forward and took the trophy from Mr. Peterson.

''Congratulations, son,'' Mr. Peterson said. ''I hope we'll see you and your teammates playing junior high soccer next year.''

Scott smiled and held the trophy over his head while the team cheered.

After the ceremony was finished, Scott looked around to see if Mom was there. He was surprised to find Mom, Dad, and Melissa standing a few steps behind him.

''We missed your game, Scott,'' Mom said, ''but we saw you get the trophy. We're very proud of you.''

They left the gym and started walking toward the car. *I really can manage on my own,* Scott thought. *And Coach Rollins is right. I can do anything I want to.*

What is Diabetes?

D iabetes is a disease that affects the way your body uses food. It causes the amount of sugar in your blood to be much too high. It also prevents your body from getting energy from your food.

To help you understand what diabetes is, you need to know the basics of how the body makes energy from the foods you eat.

Usually, during digestion, the body changes food into a form of sugar called glucose. Glucose is the fuel your body uses for energy. A body without glucose is like a car without gasoline.

Glucose travels through the bloodstream to millions of body cells. With the help of insulin, glucose enters the cells, where it is used for quick energy, or stored for later use. Insulin acts like a key that opens the doors of the cells to let glucose in. Where does the insulin come from? It is produced in the beta cells of the pancreas, a small organ that lies behind the stomach.

This process of using food for energy is crucial. The body depends on food for every action, from pumping blood, to walking, to thinking.

In diabetes, something goes wrong with this normal process of using food for energy. Food is changed into glucose easily enough, but there is a problem with insulin. In type I diabetes (the type that occurs most often in children and young adults), the pancreas cannot make any insulin. In type II diabetes (the type that occurs most often later in life), the pancreas makes some insulin, but either it doesn't make enough, or it makes insulin that the body cannot use properly (or both).

No matter which type of diabetes you have, the result is that glucose cannot be used by your body cells for energy. This is because insulin acts like a key to open the cell's lock. If insulin is not present or is not working, glucose is "locked out" of the cells and cannot be used.

So, in people with diabetes, glucose builds up in the blood. High blood-glucose levels are the major symptom of untreated diabetes. And the key to living well with diabetes is keeping those blood-glucose levels as close to normal (nondiabetic levels) as possible.

People with type I diabetes are treated with daily insulin injections, diet (a balanced meal plan that limits foods high in sugar and fat), and regular exercise. People with type II diabetes are treated with a meal plan and exercise, but if diet and exercise alone do not control blood sugar, pills or insulin may also be prescribed.

To measure blood-sugar levels, people with diabetes perform self-monitoring of blood glucose. These blood tests, done by pricking the finger for a drop of blood, measure blood-glucose levels at the moment of the test.

A second type of test, urine tests, are very useful in measuring ketones. Ketones are a waste product that the body produces when it burns fat for energy. If the body is burning fat for energy, it could mean that a person is not getting enough insulin. Ketones can appear in the urine when diabetes is not well controlled or when a person with diabetes is ill or under great stress. Ketones are a warning sign that the body is in trouble and needs help. People with diabetes work out plans for handling ketones with their doctors.

For more information about diabetes, contact your local affiliate of the American Diabetes Association—see the white pages of your phone book.

About the Author

Judy Miller lives in Bismarck, North Dakota, with her husband Ray and their two teenage sons, Mark and Alan. Ms. Miller has worked as an English teacher, and now works as a freelance writer, housewife, and volunteer for the American Diabetes Association. Ms. Miller is an active member of the ADA North Dakota Affiliate, and is currently the state public information chairperson for the Affiliate.

Other ADA Publications

Kids Corner
The mini-magazine just for kids with diabetes. It's colorful, easy-to-read, makes learning fun, and answers the questions kids are afraid to ask. Order your one-year set today! (Winter, Spring, Summer, and Fall) *#122*
Nonmember: $4.00; Member: $3.20 (Add $1.00 for shipping/handling.)

Diabetes: A to Z
This not-so-ordinary diabetes dictionary explains all of those confusing words surrounding diabetes — all in easy-to-understand terms. It answers your questions about lifestyle, nutrition, exercise, and much more. Get your own copy to browse through and another copy for a friend. #121
Nonmember: $6.95; Member: $5.55 (Add $1.75 for shipping/handling.)

Publications Catalog — Free
This catalog describes all the latest publications from the American Diabetes Association — for both the person with diabetes and the health-care team. Just indicate on your order that you want your own free copy.

To place your order, make your check or money order payable to the American Diabetes Association, Attn: Order Dept., 1660 Duke St., Alexandria, VA 22314. Be sure to include the item number, title, quantity, price, shipping/handling, and total for each publication you order. To take advantage of the Member Price, indicate your membership number (on your DIABETES FORECAST label) on the order. Prices are subject to change without notice. Allow 6 to 8 weeks for delivery.

For More Information

The American Diabetes Association (ADA) is the nation's leading voluntary health organization dedicated to improving the well-being of all people with diabetes and their families. Equally important is our unceasing support for research to find a preventive and cure for this chronic disease, which affects some 11 million Americans. The American Diabetes Association provides information and support for those who have the disease, and educates health-care professionals and the general public about the seriousness of diabetes. The Association carries out this important mission through the efforts of thousands of volunteers working at affiliates and chapters in more than 800 communities across the United States.

ADA membership puts you in contact with a network of more than 225,000 caring people in communities like yours. Our local affiliates and chapters offer services you can't find anywhere else, such as support groups, educational programs, counseling, and special camps for kids with diabetes. In addition, we publish a variety of materials for people of every age group on topics of importance not only to the individual with diabetes but to the entire family as well. Membership in your local ADA affiliate carries with it many benefits, including a subscription to

Diabetes Forecast, our lively patient education magazine, published monthly. The American Diabetes Association also distributes a free quarterly newsletter. To obtain membership information or to order the newsletter, contact the Association at the address below. To find your local affiliate, look in the white pages of your phone directory, or contact:

American Diabetes Association®, Inc.
Diabetes Information Service Center
1660 Duke Street
Alexandria, VA 22314
Tel: 800-ADA-DISC (800-232-3472)
(in VA and Washington, D.C., 703-549-1500)